# THE
# TAO
## OF
# SPORTS

# THE
# TAO
## OF
# SPORTS

BOB MITCHELL

Frog, Ltd.
Berkeley, California

*The Tao of Sports*

Published by Frog, Ltd.

Frog, Ltd. books are distributed by
North Atlantic Books
P.O. Box 12327
Berkeley, CA 94712

Cover and book design by Paula Morrison

Printed in the United States of America

**Library of Congress Cataloging-in-Publication Data**

Mitchell, Robert L., 1944–
      The tao of sports / Bob Mitchell : foreword by Stephen
Mitchell.
            p.   cm.
      ISBN 1-883319-56-0
      1. Sports.   1. Tao.   I. Title.
      GV706'02  dc21                                          96-49859
                                                             CIP

            1   2   3   4   5   6   7   8   9 / 00   99   98   97

*For Nat and Irma Mitchell*

# CONTENTS

# FOREWORD

I won't pretend that I'm not prejudiced in favor of my brother's free, imaginative, and totally wonderful adaptation of the *Tao Te Ching*. It strikes just the right tone for a sacred text about sports: breezy, funny, practical, ironic when it needs to be, never on stilts or behind a pulpit, a *Tao Te Ching* that wears jeans and talks with a slight Brooklyn accent. It probably won't make many Taoists into sports fanatics. But it may make many sports fanatics realize that they are already closet Taoists.

*Tao Te Ching* (pronounced, more or less, *"dow deh jing"*) can be translated as *The Book of the Way and of How It Manifests Itself in the World*. Its legendary author, Lao-tzu, may have lived in the sixth century B.C.E. or may not have lived at all. It doesn't really matter who wrote it or who put it together. What matters is the book: the classic manual on the art of living and one of the wonders of the world. In eighty-one brief chapters, the *Tao Te Ching* looks at the basic predicament of being alive and gives advice that imparts balance and perspective, a serene and generous spirit. It teaches how to work for the good with the effortless skill that comes from being in accord with the Tao (the basic principle of the universe) and applies equally to good government and sexual love, to child rearing, business, and ecology.

It is particularly appropriate to have a *Tao of Sports*, because sports provides many of us with our first and strongest conscious experience of being "in the Tao" or "in the zone," in the current of energy where the right action happens by itself, effortlessly. Somehow the innate intelligence of the body takes over: the ball throws the ball, the racquet swings the racquet.

This is always a magical experience. It can't be summoned by the will, and there is no formula for it. If you think about it, you lose it. It comes and goes at its own pleasure. When it comes, we are thrilled and grateful. When it is gone, we try to do our ordinary best.

It may seem odd at first to think of sports as a paradigm for life. But any part of human activity, as in a hologram, contains the whole. And it may be easier to learn the essential wisdom life has to teach us by paying closer attention to an activity that we passionately love. Wisdom is already there, in the perfect drop shot, in the blown lay-up; all we have to do is take the time to notice it. If only the lessons of life were as clear as the lessons of sports. But they are!

Listen to the spirit of Lao-tzu in its latest incarnation, speaking through the voice of Bob Mitchell, passionate sports fanatic and attentive student of the Tao.

—Stephen Mitchell

# INTRODUCTION

Some things were just meant to be.

Take this book.

Simply put, two phenomena that occurred during my life-time have conspired in the conception and writing of *The Tao of Sports*. The first has been happening since the initial tri-mester of 1944, when I was just a fetus. It was to that period that I have traced my unwavering, unquenchable passion for sports. (Although I didn't begin my baseball-card collection until eight or nine years later, I'm convinced that I was read-ing box scores over—or through—my mother's shoulder dur-ing the early stages of her pregnancy.)

The second happened when I first laid eyes on my brother's brilliant translation of Lao-tzu's *Tao Te Ching*. Prior to that reading, there was only a handful of other writers who had elicited in me the same profound feeling that can only be characterized by the word *astonishment:* Shakespeare, Poe, Dostoevsky, Mallarmé, Rilke. During my first reading of the *Tao Te Ching* (and my second and third and hundredth, for that matter), I was struck by the utter simplicity, beauty, prac-ticality, and wisdom of language and message.

Further, I realized that at some point, I had begun read-ing the text through the prism of my own personal sporting experiences. With some surprise, I began to see that it all fit, that the lessons from the Tao that could be applied to life could equally be applied, beautifully and with almost uncanny consistency, to all the nooks and crannies of sports. That every chapter of this ancient text corresponds to problems, chal-lenges, and situations confronted by the modern athlete. (I have, in fact, replaced the original "numbers" with specific chapter titles.) And that many of the questions I had posed while following and participating in sports during my fifty-one years (plus, of course, the fetal period) were answered, thanks to Lao-tzu and my brother.

What has resulted from the confluence of these two passionate experiences is a book that takes the basic themes and rhythms of the *Tao Te Ching* and transposes them, in my own language, to the specific arena of sports. A book that, as an antidote to all the recent attention being showered on the underbelly of sports (grandstanding, violence, incivility, greed), can have us all thinking instead about issues like humility, respect, balance, and compassion. And also, ideally, a book that human beings intensely involved in sports and life will find helpful, perhaps inspirational, in their continuing pursuit and understanding of self-knowledge and excellence.

# AUTHOR'S NOTE

In a number of chapters, I refer to the athlete (or the "true athlete") alternately as "he" or "she." This is not a reflection of my desire to avoid the unwieldy "he/she" expression; rather, it reflects the fact that the lessons of *The Tao of Sports* are meant equally for men and women, both of whom share this, as (virtually) every other human experience. The reader should, of course, feel free to substitute one pronoun for the other—as he/she wishes, and at his/her discretion.

# THE
# TAO
## OF
# SPORTS

# I

# MYSTERY

The Game is bigger than any game. The Game is beyond the scope of all games. It's ceaselessly fascinating, endlessly challenging. It's the crucible from which growth, learning, and self-discovery emerge. Most of all, it's inscrutable and mysterious. For starters, consider this: *the ball bounces!* This way or that, you don't know. And you'll never know. Why try to understand it? Why try to control it? Winning is one way, but that's tricky: one bad bounce, and you lose. Winning or losing isn't what it's all about anyway; it's about accepting the Game in the very depths of you. On the field, the unexpected is always just around the corner, waiting to pounce. When? Who knows. Why? Who can tell. But the wise athlete accepts it, takes pleasure in it, learns from it. Just keep your eye on the ball: wherever it may bounce, that is the true way.

# 2

# PARADOX

The Game gives, the Game takes away. You try with all your might without results; then you just hang on for the ride, and the magic happens. Opposites coexist: glory and humility, urgency and patience, power and softness, pain and joy. For each winner, there's a loser; for each loser, a winner. The true athlete accepts the fundamental paradoxes of sport. He knows that from contradiction comes growth, from conflict comes understanding. Thus, he is able to act by not acting, to move by standing still, to make noise by being silent, to accept defeat by being content.

# 3

# LOSING

I win, you lose: so this means I'm better than you? Winning and losing are impostors, posing as self-worth and inadequacy. Do you cherish winning and detest losing? Do you think you're better or worse as a person, depending upon the result? Fact is, you're no better or worse than the fullness of your effort, than the focus and dedication and enthusiasm with which you play. If you only chase victory and fear defeat, you'll never attain balance and hold to the center. Case in point: despite his huge mound of victories, Cy Young also lost more games than any other pitcher *ever*. The Game has a way of evening things out. It is the Game, not winning the game, that will ultimately bring you satisfaction. And losing comes not from losing, but from missing out on the learning and the growth and the challenge.

# 4

# POSSIBILITIES

In sports, anything can happen! You're digging in at the plate or barking signals at the line of scrimmage or taking it out of bounds or addressing the ball or preparing to serve or crouched at the starting line. Now take a deep breath, and what do you see? Isn't the playing field level, waiting to be tipped? Isn't the result still in doubt, regardless of the odds? Isn't the potential for anything to happen hovering, prepared to be exploited? Nothing is ever certain, except that nothing is ever impossible. Every moment is unique and full of possibilities, a renewal of the struggle, a fresh start. Sports is not just what is, but continually what might be. There is no feat that can't be performed, no act that can't be executed, no underdog that can't be victorious, no favorite that can't be upset. Which explains why Clay flogged Liston and the U.S. outskated Russia and Fleck upset Hogan and the Miners surprised the Wildcats and Riggs unsettled Court and the Mets shocked the O's and the Jets upended the Colts and you can achieve anything.

# 5

# JUSTICE

The Game has its own rules, not those you ascribe to it. Results happen, not because they *should* but because they *do*. The Game doesn't take sides; it doesn't always reward you with victory or defeat for playing well or badly. Playing well is its own reward. Things balance out in the end, all in good time: you can do nothing to control this. So: take your defeats with equanimity, accept your victories with humility. With no expectations, there's no disappointment. Since the Game is mysterious and has its own agenda, you don't deserve to win: *you win*. You aren't destined to lose: *you lose*. When you realize *this* system of justice, you'll always hold your head high, whatever the outcome.

# 6

# INFINITY

The bad news: your body has limits—weight, height, strength, endurance, speed, power. The good news: your heart and your spirit don't. They carry with them the possibility of infinite potential, infinite resilience, infinite achievement. They reach where arms and feet can't, find flexibility that hips and neck don't, can be pushed when thighs and torso won't. Wherever you go, you carry around your own private reservoirs of passion, fortitude, and persistence right there inside of you. And if you let them, they can lead you wherever you wish to go.

# 7

# DETACHMENT

Consider *this* surprising paradox: let the Game play itself! Do you want to control things but can't? Let go. Do you worry about results? Let go. Do you care about the judgment of others? Let go. If you take the Game by the throat, you'll end up strangling your own efforts. If you let it breathe slowly and peacefully, you'll find serenity and satisfaction. Put your whole heart into your effort, then let go. Invest your whole self in the spirit of the Game, and it will repay you in full.

# 8

# PASSION

W hy do you compete? To win? To dominate? To prove your worthiness or assert your manliness? All these require passion, but passion has two edges: one motivates, the other consumes. Direct your passion inwards. Compare yourself not to others, but to yourself. Channel your passion not against your opponent or toward winning at any cost, but rather toward excelling, uniting body and mind, discovering your potential, expressing yourself fully, making yourself the best you can be. The true athlete plays the Game for its own sake, directing his passion inside himself so that he may discover who he is.

# 9

# INDEPENDENCE

What importance do you attach to the Game? Do you place too high a value on winning and losing? (Do they reflect who you are or how you feel?) Do you judge yourself by your performance? (Do you rest on your laurels or dwell on your mistakes?) Do you look to others for approval? (Do you depend on them to confirm your worthiness?) Do you watch the scoreboard? (Does the performance of others affect yours?) The Game isn't attached to anything but itself. It has no meaning, no message, no consequences. Play it with everything you've got, let it fill your heart with joy. Then go home, take a nice hot shower, and get on with your life.

# 10

# FLOW

Ebbing and flowing continually, the Game is like a great ocean. Like water, it can't be stopped or controlled or redirected or possessed by the human hand or mind. Its movement can't be dictated or changed: it *is*. Be aware of your place in this movement, take part in and enjoy its subtle rhythms. Every point, every shot, every moment is part of a continuum, a stepping stone, a bridge. Like an ocean's waves, there's always a next one. Compete from within, without expectations, accepting that whatever you do will have its effect on the whole in some way; the rest will take care of itself. Step back, let events take their course. Swim against the current and you'll drown. Swim with it and it will carry you wherever you're going.

# II

# INTANGIBLES

How can you judge an athlete's worth based on statistics alone? Are there statistics for trying? Are there numbers that measure heart or courage or tenacity? Do results on the outside reflect satisfaction on the inside? If you hold the guy you're guarding scoreless, does it appear in the box score? What about all the unheralded acts: perfect pivots, successful bunts, balls blocked in the dirt? Aces are great, but what about service returns? And shouldn't performing when it counts, with the pressure on, count twice as much as at other times? Can a brilliant career cut short by injury and marked by modest numbers prevent the fieriest competitor from entering the Panthcon? When you judge yourself, do you look at scores and records, or qualities that no one else can see? Woody Hayes said it best: *Statistics always remind me of the guy who drowned in the river whose average depth was only three feet.*

# OPENNESS

L ike plants, athletes grow and flourish when they're open. Desires cloud your focus; feelings blunt your effort; thoughts inhibit your instincts. The true athlete is open to the present moment, receives what the Game has to give. The past is of no consequence: *should have, could have, would have* don't count. The future can't be controlled: expectations sap your strength and dilute your effort. All that exists is what *is*. So: step up to the plate or the tee-box or the service line or the foul line or the starting line or the blue line or the line of scrimmage. And let it happen!

# 13

# IMPOSTORS

Over the archway outside the men's locker room at Wimbledon appears the Kipling quote: *If you can meet with triumph and disaster / And treat those two impostors just the same. . . .* How many times do you think: *I hope I win?* Or: *I'm afraid to lose?* Winning, losing, hope, fear: the villains of the sporting theater. Results parade as friends or foes; expectations cloud the moment. Now consider this: how long do the pleasure and pain of winning and losing last? If a single play leaves you with joy or frustration, what about the next one? If the next one does the same, what about the one after that? And after all those plays, and the game turns out one way or another, the happiness or grief will last until . . . the next game. And after all those games, and the season turns out one way or another, the smiles or frowns will last until . . . the first play of the first game of the next season. What *will* last are your passion for excelling and the joys of competition. Trust in the challenge of the Game and in your own best efforts: that is your job as an athlete, and as a person.

# 14

# ANARCHY

On the surface, the Game seems tidy and knowable, with its guidelines and rules and regulations: imagine what it would be without them! As it is, it's still pretty chaotic. Nothing can be taken for granted: plans, formulas, and strategies are fine, but what happens once that crazy ball is actually set in motion? The instant you dare to anticipate . . . SURPRISE! Count on results, and in the blink of an eye things go haywire. The Game has no rhyme or reason, so you can never know it: all you can do is play it.

# 15

# PATIENCE

You're behind by fifteen with seven minutes to go. You've lost the first set in a tiebreaker. You can't find your breaking stuff. So what? Take a breath, trust yourself and the flow of the Game, be alert and receptive, see what happens. Whatever the situation, take things as they come, without forcing the issue. In the heat of the moment, there's always time for coolness. With patience, the most serious mistakes can be corrected, the most obvious trends reversed, the largest deficits erased. A Chinese proverb says it: *Patience, and the mulberry leaf becomes a silk gown.*

# 16

# SERENITY

The athlete who merely tries to win puffs herself up like a bullfrog, wishing to intimidate, putting her ego ahead of her effort. The athlete who understands the Game is humbled by it, its greatness, its complexity, its mystery. You can never solve or conquer it. Sometimes you come close and fall under the delusion of control: the odd hole-in-one or perfect drop volley or miraculous fingertip snare. But the Game teaches you to humble yourself in its presence, to find peace and serenity in your smallness, to be constantly vigilant for victory but to be always prepared for defeat. The athlete who truly appreciates the Game will begin to appreciate her true place in the universe.

# 17

# LEADERSHIP

To be a player is hard enough. But to *lead* other players is the ultimate paradox. For captain, manager, or coach, it means being present yet invisible. Allowing players to perform on their terms, not yours. Demonstrating, not describing. Lecturing without talking. Trusting so that trust is returned. Teaching so that you might learn. Developing technique, knowledge, and confidence, then disappearing into thin air. Unless, of course, you prefer to buy into Casey's theory: *The secret of managing is to keep the five guys who hate you away from the five guys who are undecided.*

# 18

# ANONYMITY

Sporting accomplishment has no name. Where *great* is used, complacency may follow. Where *best* asserts itself, false pride can't be far behind. Where *number one* is applied, delusion is likely to hover. And besides, how long do accomplishments last? Hole-in-one may be followed by triple-bogey; ace by double-fault; game-winning homer by bases-loaded strikeout; winning jumper at the buzzer by missed free-throw with the game on the line; TD pass by fumble; turkey by 7-10 split; winning by losing. Believe in yourself, prepare, work hard, give it your all. Then sit back, and let the pundits call you whatever they like.

# 19

# CENTER

The way to find peace in sports is to hold to the center. Keep your mind focused on balance and consistency, and do what feels comfortable. Know yourself, your strengths and weaknesses, and you'll always find your way. Think about it: is it mere chance that everything begins and ends at the center? Strength down the middle is the baseball standard. (Why did they position the mound in the center of everything?) Without football's center, no play would ever occur. (Why did they put the quarterback at the *real* center?) With few exceptions, great basketball teams begin at the center. (Why did they place the most dominant player in the middle?) In golf, if you keep it down the middle, you'll never shoot over 90. (Why do they have most hazards on the sides?) In tennis, the trick is to keep returning to the center. (Why do points usually end when someone is out of position?) Keep your mind and heart and body at the center of things, and you'll always find yourself balanced, with your feet firmly on the ground.

# 20

# NON-THOUGHT

*Grip your club nice and loose. Bend your knees. Line up your thumbs. Line up your feet. Keep your head down. Keep your head still. Keep your right arm close to your body. Keep an arc on your backswing. Keep your club parallel to the ground. Bend your left knee. Turn your hips. Drive your left side through. Pronate your right hand. Turn your left foot. Turn your right foot. Keep your head down. Follow through until your club is again parallel to the ground.* When the brain is too full, the heart is neglected. When the mind is too occupied, the body is distracted. Don't overthink things. If you do, thoughts will interfere with performance: fear, doubt, self-consciousness, failure, even perfection. Clear your mind, and let your body take over. Eliminate your plans, and let your natural rhythms flow. Don't worry about results, and they'll happen in spite of yourself. Or, as Yogi once put it, *How can you think and hit at the same time?*

# SELF-ESTEEM

All you need to play the Game, to be fulfilled by it, to extract joy from it, can be found in one place. Not on the outside, but within. Sure, applause and adulation are nice, but don't let them drown out your inner voice. Accolades and approval are fine, but depend on your native instincts. You are your own most loyal fan, your own most insightful critic, your own most gifted teacher. So that if you experience defeat, you won't waver in your belief in yourself and your abilities, nor will you doubt your effort. Feel good about yourself, perform up to your *own* standards, then go to bed with a smile on your lips.

# 22

# MODESTY

The true athlete has nothing to prove. She does her job with no ulterior motives, no hidden agendas. Her only goals are excellence, putting forth her best effort, learning from her mistakes. She is aware of her place in the Game; that her successes are relative and fleeting and her failures inevitable and fleeting; that without a strong opponent, her performance is diminished; that she is part of a process, larger and more important than she alone will ever be; that she shares a love of competing with countless others who have gone before her, who strive with her, and who are yet to follow her. And so, she doesn't judge herself in terms of stature or greatness, even though she may stand above everyone else.

# 23

# TRUST

Without trust, there's no contentment, only fear and insecurity. Trust in the Game and its wisdom, and only good can happen. Trust in your inner voice, and only peace can exist. At the crucial moment of the game, whether you're on the mound or the green or the service line or the foul line, it's all in your hands. So what can happen? Only one thing, if there's trust: you'll do what feels right. Then, whatever the outcome, you'll know the serenity that comes from having surrendered to something greater than yourself. (By the way, this technique works every time. Trust me.)

# 24

# FREEDOM

Imagine what it would be like to depend on nothing! To be unattached to the past or the future, to approval or disapproval, to pressure or fear, to demands or expectations, to controlling or being controlled. The Game should be played with total freedom: the true athlete abandons herself to the dictates of her body, her instincts, her creativity. She doesn't think about or cling to anything outside herself, but rather lets go of everything, giving herself up to the rhythm of the moment. With no agendas. No plans. No one to please. Nothing to prove.

# RESPECT

There are two ways of perceiving what is greater than you: fear and respect. You fear what you don't understand, respect what you do. Like the lion and the shark, the Game, when understood, commands respect; when not, it invites fear. Understand your opponent in order to respect his efforts. Appreciate your place in the Game in order to respect its process. Study the Game's history in order to respect your predecessors. Learn the Game's nuances in order to respect its difficulty. Try to know the Game, in all its complexity and challenge, and you'll never fear inadequacy or defeat.

# 26

# ROOTS

How tempting to swim in the twin pools of expectation and adventure! But: if you give in to the allure of the future, you'll lose your focus on the moment. If you yield too easily to the call of the unknown, you'll stray from what you know well. Keep to your roots, to what you do with excellence and consistency, to what got you to where you are now. Above all, return to the fundamentals you can perform by heart, depend on the basic executions you can summon up without thinking. Yes: expand, adapt, improvise, create when the moment calls for it; but find comfort in getting back to the basics when you need to. And never forget: without roots, you'd also be toothless, and there'd be no flowers in your garden.

# 27

# HEART

The heart is the center of the true athlete. Sure, legs and arms and brain are all essential, but the heart is *the* defining body part. Defining, yet indefinable. It's the source of passion, courage, creativity, intuition. It permits the unplanned, the spontaneous, the unexpected moment. It allows for heroism in the human spirit: *keep on trying, never give up.* From nowhere and with no reason, it creates surprise, wonder, electricity, magic. The French philosopher Blaise Pascal hit the nail on the head: *The heart has its reasons which Reason doesn't have a clue about.*

# 28

# EQUIPMENT

Like a bad carpenter, an insecure athlete blames her tools. Doesn't a racquet simply serve as an extension of your swing? Don't a club and a bat merely obey the movements of your arms and legs and hips? Isn't a ball truly democratic, bouncing equally for all? Focus on your movement, your positioning, your timing, your coordination, your concentration, your relaxation. Rely on your natural abilities and instincts, and your equipment won't betray you. And if you still don't agree, how in the world do you explain the fact that the old Italian clay-court specialist Beppe Merlo used to beat up on bigger opponents while using a racquet with a red children's handle and strung at thirty pounds?

# 29

# PERFECTION

There's no such animal as perfection in sports: the most perfect of games is always flawed. In his '56 Series gem, Larsen made a few bad pitches and needed some defensive help. In the '73 NCAA finals, Walton missed one shot from the field (oh yeah: he also canned 21). During his 59, Geiberger misread a putt or two. In the '74 U.S. Open finals, Connors dominated totally but still lost two games. At best, the athlete's performance is awe-inspiring, courageous, noble: it is never perfect. Only the Game is.

# 30

# SELF-ACCEPTANCE

The ordinary athlete looks for approval from others; the true athlete seeks it from within. When you accept yourself, the Game accepts you as well. If you're comfortable with yourself, there's no need to dominate or control. If you know who you are, there's no need to force the issue. The athlete who accepts only her strengths is limited. The one who also accepts her limits is strong. If your curveball isn't working, pick your spots with the fastball. If your jumper's off, work on your passing. If you can't serve-and-volley, develop your topspin lob and passing shot. If you're short off the tee, keep it on the fairway. As long as you listen to your inner voice, there's no need to look outside for help. The Latin satirist Persius summed it up: *Don't seek yourself outside yourself.*

# 31

# COMPASSION

D o you see your opponent as your enemy? Do you suspect his motives? Do you underestimate his worth? If so, you'll end up disliking, mistrusting, and overestimating yourself. He's your mirror: he's striving for what you're striving for, using the same tools, working just as hard to prepare, to perform. His spirit, like yours, is committed; he brings out the best in you, just as you push him to higher levels. Win or lose, you share a common bond. Feel compassion toward him, and you feel empathy toward yourself. Respect him, and you respect your own efforts. It's a rare yet universal feeling that touches all who compete in earnest: Arnie and Jack, Chris and Martina, Jackie and Sal, Pelé and Eusebio, C.K. and Rafer, Carmen and Sugar Ray, Wilt and Bill. You and your opponent.

# 32

# LIMITS

Passion and limits: again, the paradox of sports! Go all out, give it all you've got, just do it; on the other hand, know when to step back, when to pace yourself, even when to stop. Get to know your limits. How far can you go before you can't go any more? How long can you drive yourself before you run out of gas? How daring can you be before you pay the piper? Know what you can do, and do it as well as you can. But also know what you can't do, then go back to doing what you can.

# 33

# SELF-KNOWLEDGE

Before you can begin to know the Game, you must begin to know yourself. Before you can accept losing, you must develop a sense of humility. Before you can defeat your opponent, you must learn to defeat your own demons. Ask yourself: Do I know myself well enough to trust myself always? Do I know my strengths and weaknesses well enough to know my limits? Do I know my inner resources so I can depend on them when they're needed? Do I play the Game only to win, or to improve as an athlete and grow as a person? Lao-tzu said it perfectly: *Mastering others is strength; mastering yourself is true power.*

# 34

# GREATNESS

The arrogant athlete calls himself great; the great athlete lets others do the talking. To him, greatness is not something to be pursued: it's a by-product of what he does naturally. Does the eagle brag of his grace? Does the cheetah shout, *Look how fast I can run*? Does the grizzly ask the salmon to admire the power of his claws? The athlete who strives for excellence will find it in his own way, naturally, never thinking to praise himself. He isn't aware of being superior, but rather of how he can be *better*. And this, more than his skills or his preparation or his poise, is what truly makes him great.

# 35

# PEACE

Here's an exercise for you. Imagine you're preparing for a big tennis match. (Or golf or baseball or basketball or football or hockey or soccer or squash or swimming or skiing or billiards or bowling or tiddlywinks or whatever.) There'll be lots of outside pressure to perform well, even to win. You've put in all the painful hours of preparation, done all you could to get your game in shape. You'll never be readier, and the prospect of playing at your best is exciting. It's just before the match (or the game or the meet or whatever). Now close your eyes and let the feeling of peace envelop your body and mind. You're feeling good, and you're going to give it everything you've got. Whatever pain or discomfort you'll feel while playing will be overcome by this incredible sense of peace and harmony within yourself. Whether your efforts result in victory or defeat won't matter either, won't affect your inner calm and poise. O.K., now open your eyes. Feel better?

# 36

# COUNTERPOINT

The sixty-four-million-dollar question: *Do power and aggressiveness always win in sports?* The sixty-four-million-dollar answer: *No!* Like paper covering rock in that old "rock-paper-scissors" game, power can be absorbed, aggressiveness stifled. He serves a cannonball? You use his pace to chip a return at his feet. He throws a 96-mph fastball? You meet the ball and use his speed to stroke it back through the box. He barrels down the lane, head down, for a lay-up? You stand your ground and take a charge. Power and aggressiveness are nice to have, but reacting to them is even nicer. Which is how soft can overcome hard, contact can blunt speed, positioning can overcome force. React instinctively to your opponent's efforts and *he'll* be the one huffing and puffing.

# 37

# HARMONY

Learn to appreciate the difference between joy and desires. Joy is free, unfettered by motive, and results from the simple pleasures of excelling, of competing. Desires are ego-based: the wanting to please, the conscious wishing to avoid failure. Joy produces natural rhythms; desires create stress and tension. Walk serenely on a balance beam placed on the floor, then raise it six feet in the air. Or hit a cozy bucket of balls by yourself, then tee one up on the first tee with your boss and thirty others watching. Or have a leisurely catch with your friend, then trot in as a reliever in the bottom of the ninth with the score tied, the bases loaded, and an inherited two-and-oh count. Free yourself from desires, from the worry and the consciousness of failure and results: the only path to inner peace and harmony.

# 38

# ACHIEVEMENT

What is the feeling of achievement? Is it holding a trophy aloft? Or seeing four-for-four after your name in a box score? Or breaking a record or beating your nemesis? All these are fine, but in the long run they'll trickle through your fingers like water. Achievement you can grasp at or reach for or see doesn't last; achievement you try to attain doesn't always come. True achievement is deeper and comes when it comes, without your beckoning or coaxing. *Try* to achieve, and chances are you won't. Try simply to compete and to excel, and achievement will come in time. You may not be able to see it or touch it or hold it in your hands. It may not have your name engraved on it. But when it sneaks up behind you and taps you gently on the shoulder, you'll know who it is.

# 39

# RENEWAL

The wonderful thing about sports: there's always a next time! A next at-bat, an extra inning, a second serve, another point, another down, another hole, another tournament, a new half, a new game, a new season. So if at first you don't succeed, you get another chance. And if at first you *do* succeed, you get another chance anyway. A chance to forget about the past, to not worry about the future, to focus on the moment, to bounce back, to start all over. Think about it: how often in life are you given the chance to get so many do-overs?

# 40

# YIELDING

Next time you see a "YIELD" sign, remember this: if you play the Game by the rules and let the other guy make the mistakes and give a little without giving up, chances are you'll avoid any serious accidents.

# 41

# STRUGGLE

Once upon a time, long ago, in a faraway kingdom, there lived a glorious athlete for whom everything came easily. He didn't have to put in hours of conditioning to make his body hard and his mind tough. He didn't have to undergo tediously repetitive practice sessions. He didn't have to develop his skills painstakingly, since they were already fully honed from the beginning. When he competed, so great was his prowess that he found his opponents rarely pushed him or made him try harder or drove him to reach higher levels of performance. And since he always won handily, he never experienced the pleasures of a hard-fought battle, the sweetness of coming from behind to win, or the joy of the struggle that leads to total physical and spiritual satisfaction. Obviously, this is a fairy tale.

# 42

## SOLITUDE

Yet another paradox of sports: the more you embrace your solitude, the closer you become to something a lot larger than yourself. Is it lonely out there on the mound? Or on the green? Or at the service line or the foul line or the line of scrimmage? If you embrace your solitude and view it as a personal opportunity, you also embrace the situation itself, your opponent, your special niche in time and space, and all those who have shared, are sharing, and will share this same experience in this same situation. In fact, you're embracing tradition, the continuum of success and failure . . . the Game itself! So that no matter how alone you feel, you always have plenty of company.

# 43

# GENTLENESS

So the Wind was bragging to the Sun that he alone could make the man shed his overcoat. But the harder he blew, the tighter the man clung to the coat. Finally, he gave up, and the Sun came out and simply shined. And—lo and behold!—off came the garment. To shine in sports, sometimes it's better to take the gentler route. That's precisely why you have at your disposal: the drop shot and the touch volley, the sacrifice bunt and the sneaky slider, the screen pass and the coffin-corner punt, the deke and the touch pass, the finger-roll and the tip-in, the feathered bunker shot and the delicate eight-foot, downhill, cross-grain, two-foot-left-to-right-breaking, all-pace putt. All (shining) examples of how finesse can overshadow fury, savvy can negate aggressiveness, and gentleness can humble strength.

# 44

# JOY

Here's a no-brainer for you: all you have to do to find joy in the Game is to play it. Nothing to think about: *just play!* Nothing to analyze: *just play!* And best of all: there's joy even in the littlest of things. How sweet it is just to feel the texture of the ash in your hands while you're waiting for the next pitch. How satisfying to catch a drop volley just right and watch it die ever-so-gently on the other side of the net. Of the five bunkers you land in during your round, there's probably one where you hit exactly two inches behind your ball, then watch in amazement as it follows a rooster-tail of sand on its merry way to the hole. What a thrill to experience the feeling accompanying that bounce pass (you know, the one where you thread the needle between two opponents right to your teammate breaking toward the basket). To say nothing of the intense pleasure of making that perfect tackle, that 7–10 split, that three-cushion kiss, that penalty shot in the top corner, that unexpected dink. At some point, sooner or later, and (if you practice enough) more frequently than you think, the joy of sports is there for the taking, available to everyone in the universe, twenty-four hours a day, seven days a week!

# 45

# ARTLESSNESS

True artists are invisible. They create their works, and when they're finished, they disappear into the paint or the marble or the notes or the words. Such is the way of the true athlete: a vehicle traveling through space, she lets the Game play itself. She doesn't let her will or her reason or her ego interfere with the flow; rather, she is dissolved into it. With total surrender comes total freedom. So that even while she's trying with all her might, her work seems effortless.

# 46

# FEAR

The athlete who truly loves the Game has no fear in her heart. Since it's an illusion, it will disappear in the face of joy and enthusiasm. Like water thrown on the Wicked Witch of the West, throw passion on your fear, make it vanish with your commitment. *(It's melting! It's melting!)* So what's there to fear? Your opponent? Not if you see her as an ally who's striving for the same things you are, rather than as your enemy. Failure? Not if you accept your efforts and their consequences, come what may. The loss of your pride? Not if you know your limits, your shortcomings. The disapproval of others? Not if you believe in yourself. The damaging of your self-respect? Not if you love the Game unconditionally and appreciate your place in it.

# 47

# UNCONSCIOUSNESS

You can't package it or summon it by the force of your will or your logic or your intelligence. It comes and goes as it pleases. When you have it, you know it but don't know why. It can't be explained or understood, but it has been experienced by every single person who has ever laced up a sneaker. It can be called the "zone" or the "Tao." It's when your racquet or club or feet or hands seem to have a life of their own, guided by some magical force. It has been best described in the following way: *He was un-conscious*. And he was!

# 48

# NON-ACTION

The Game ain't broke, so why fix it? It has a mind of its own, so why try to out-think it? Non-action doesn't mean just standing around doing nothing. It doesn't mean you can't change a strategy that isn't working or correct your errors. It means not interfering with the Game, its rhythms, its workings. It means letting things take their course, naturally, without pressing or forcing the situation. It's like trying to conceive a child or to write a poem: the more you try consciously to make it happen, the harder it is to do.

# 49

# PURITY

Love the Game when you win, love it when you lose: this is true love. Feel compassion toward your teammates, feel it toward your opponents: this is true compassion. Trust yourself when you're in the zone, and when you're in a slump: this is true trust. Respect the Game when the ball bounces straight, and when it bounces funny: this is true respect. Never give up, even when losing seems certain: this is true tenacity. Believe in yourself, even when others don't: this is true poise. The Game isn't kind to fair-weather friends but is a real friend to the athlete who is true.

# 50

# LABOR

It helps the athlete to have: physical ability, natural talent, passion, a love for the Game, lots of savvy and experience, poise, the ability to focus, patience, discipline, finesse, tenacity, marvelous instincts, a great attitude, and the heart of a lion. None of which is worth very much if he isn't willing to put in all those tedious, repetitive, and painful hours practicing his sport. Coach Wooden said it best: *Nothing will work unless you do.*

# 51

# SELF-EXPRESSION

One of the great gifts the Game offers you every time you lace up the sneakers or spikes or skates: the ability to express yourself! Your wind-up, your free-throw, your spiral, your slap-shot, your serve, your dribble, your stride, your stroke, your rhythm, your swing, your pivot, your stance, your movement, your carriage; each one belongs to you and you alone. Each is unique, resembling no other—your fingerprint, your personal signature! So that, win or lose, you're not simply performing; you're actually depositing your John Hancock on the blank parchment of competition.

# 52

# INSIGHT

If you play the Game just to see who gets more points, you're missing the point. When the dust settles and the ball stops bouncing, look at all you've learned: how to profit from experience, how to develop poise and resilience, how to handle adversity, how to handle success, how to manage stress, how to work and play well with others! And most of all, an understanding of who you are and how you can be better. You can never stop learning from the Game, no matter how long you play. Or, as Coach Wooden put it: *It's what you learn, after you know it all, that counts.*

# 53

# BALANCE

A time for risk, a time for caution. (Go for the ace? Spin the ball in safely?) A time for bravado, a time for sacrifice. (Go for the fences? Move the runner along?) A time for glory, a time for humility. (Go for the 58-yarder? Punt and let the defense give you a reprieve?) A time for urgency, a time for patience. (Thread the needle through the pines? Pitch out safely and take your lumps?) As with Nature, sports has its own delicate balance: if you tamper with it, it'll go out of kilter. If you respect it, it'll reward you with its mystery and its beauty. Keep to the center, remain within yourself, learn when it's best to do what, and you'll find your way. *Nothing in excess.* Such was the lesson of the Oracle. Such is the lesson of the Game.

# 54

# HONOR

And the Game appeared from above, decreeing that whosoever shall play it shall abide by these ten commandments: 1. Thou shalt not transgress the rules of the Game. 2. Thou shalt not cast aspersions upon thine opponent. 3. Thou shalt not cast aspersions upon thine umpire. 4. Thou shalt honor thy linesman and thy referee. 5. Thou shalt refrain from bitching and moaning. 6. Thou shalt not call a ball out if thou dost not really, really see it. 7. Thou shalt hit the ball where it lyeth, without giving thyself a preferred lie. 8. Thou shalt never, ever sandbag. 9. Thou shalt not commit excuses. 10. Thou shalt not covet thy neighbor's trophies.

# 55

# DISAPPOINTMENT

S o what happens when you do the best you possibly can
... and lose? Are you disappointed with the result? With
the fact that you didn't come out on top? That despite
your best efforts, you failed? Have you considered the fact
that on this day, your opponent might have been better? Or
that on this day, your effort was equal to your opponent's but
someone had to win and someone had to lose, and that's the
way it turned out? If you're content with your effort and don't
expect results, you'll never be disappointed. Or, as Doris Day
chirped, *Qué sera, sera.*

# 56

# SILENCE

The four reasons any athlete opens his mouth: to complain, to harass, to brag, to take a drink. The true athlete doesn't complain because he's content with who he is. He doesn't harass because he'd rather respect his opponent than berate him. He doesn't brag because he prefers to let his determination, passion, tenacity, and poise do the talking. He does, however, get thirsty from time to time.

# SURRENDER

Another intriguing paradox of sports: how do you surrender without giving up? The Game is too complex for you to be able to "control your own destiny." It's one thing if you were playing all by yourself under perfect conditions. But add an opponent with comparable abilities, the conditions of the playing area, meteorology, and the Game's vagaries, then try to control how things go! You play the shift for the dead-pull-hitter, and he goes opposite field. Your horse isn't a "mudder," and it rains the day of the big race. You aim your wedge shot ten feet to the right of the pin, and the wind suddenly dies down. You serve an ace, and the linesman calls a foot-fault. Never give up, but surrender yourself to the ways of the Game: the recipe for athletic satisfaction.

# 58

# EFFORT

A big difference between trying and *trying*. It's one thing to try: you give it your best shot, you don't hold back, you hang in there, you never give up. Then there's *trying:* you're so close to winning you can taste it, you've *got* to make things happen, you *have* to get on base, slam that ace, can that jumper, convert that spare, hole that putt.... So: to practice concentrating on the effort itself and not the result, here's a simple exercise. Close your eyes, take a deep breath, and imagine yourself in a do-or-die pressure situation. Now, try setting your jaw without clenching your teeth.

# 59

# SUPPLENESS

The willow, able to bend in the wind, avoids breaking. Likewise, the athlete who is able to bend can survive any situation and remain in one piece. Keep your body fluid, move with the flow of the Game, bend as the situation requires. Keep your mind open, free of thoughts and desires, receptive to all possibilities. Keep your spirit free, accept good fortune and setbacks equally, make use of anything the Game brings your way. And always remember to bend your knees!

# 60

# MISFORTUNE

Look at it this way: there's no such thing as a bad bounce! The ball bounces one way or the other, and you play it or you don't. And if you don't, you move on. On the playing field, nothing bad can happen to you: misfortune is something that happens in Greek tragedies, the result of a flawed character. In sports, there's no bad luck and no good luck, just hard work and bouncing balls. Or, as Branch Rickey quipped, *Luck is the residue of design.*

# 61

# SELF-CORRECTION

From the beginning of time, anyone who has ever competed in the sporting arena has made errors, misses, mistakes, miscues, blunders, bumbles, bobbles, boners, goofs, and gaffes of one kind or another. The ordinary athlete feels guilt or shame or remorse or pain; the true athlete accepts it as part of the Game and attempts to correct herself. She practices endlessly to eliminate the deficiency. And if she happens to commit the very same error, she rededicates herself and doubles her efforts. So it doesn't hapen again.

# 62

# TENACITY

Fighting on to the bitter end, without hesitation or compromise, is the most accurate barometer of the true athlete. Win or lose, the ability to never quit, to hang on grittily until the outcome is determined, to overcome the most daunting odds and obstacles and adversity, is what truly separates man and woman from animals. Except, of course, the admirable bulldog.

# 63

# CHALLENGE

O.K. It's match point against, and you're returning the monster serve. It's the seventy-second hole, and it all depends on your 8-iron to the postage-stamp green. You're on the foul line, down by 2 with :02 to go. It's the bottom of the ninth, you're behind by one, the bases are loaded with two out, you're up, and it's oh-and-two. So what's there to fear? Inadequacy? Defeat? Failure? Don't you see that adversity is the very time when learning takes place? Would you rather give in to difficulty than profit from it? Would you rather hold back than discover who you truly are? When things seem darkest, a neon light should flash on: *hit out, let 'er rip, be daring!* Most of all, be yourself. Give yourself fully to this moment as you would to any other moment. Cherish challenge and adversity. Believe in yourself, and the Game will never disappoint you.

# 64

# POISE

In the heat of battle, when grenades are exploding all around you and the pressure is really on, here are five thoughts you might want to keep in mind: 1. *Go with what brung you to the dance. 2. Anything can happen, and always does. 3. Whatever happens, you've got your health. 4. Think positive, and don't leave anything in the bag. 5. Hey, it's only a game.*

# SIMPLICITY

H ere's a quiz for you. The simplest motion a pitcher can go into? (Hint: the no-windup.) The only per-fect World Series game ever? (Hint: Don Larsen.) The simplest way to catch a fly ball? (Hint: the basket catch.) The most efficient throw/catch motion ever? (Hint: Willie Mays ) The simplest running play you can design? (Hint: the power sweep.) The most unstoppable NFL running play ever? (Hint: the '66 Packers.) Waste not, want not: wasted motion means wasted emotion. Avoid excess and the unnecessary. Economize, and the riches of sports will jingle in your pock-ets. *Simplify, simplify*. The quote is Thoreau's. The challenge is yours.

# 66

# COMPETITION

Do you compete *with* or *against* your opponent? Is the purpose of competing simply to feel the thrill of victory (or the agony of defeat)? Or to feel the thrill of performing well and with courage (or the agony of not giving it your best effort)? At its best, the act of competing can show you (with the help of your opponent!) to what levels you're capable of performing, how you can improve yourself, exactly what you're made of. The Olympic credo sums up this spirit most eloquently: *swifter, higher, stronger*.

# 67

# INTROSPECTION

The difference between a mirror and sports: the former lets you look *at* yourself, the latter allows you to look *inside* yourself. What are your fears, your strengths, your limits, your goals, your capabilities when the going gets tough? Are you able to dig deep inside to mine your reservoirs of poise, passion, compassion, and courage? In times of stress, to what extent are you capable of tenacity, humility, resilience, and honor? The answers to these questions are often found on the field of play, when the chips are down and you have no one to answer to but yourself. Thurber said it: *All men should strive to learn before they die what they are running from, and to, and why.*

# 68

# INNOCENCE

The child is innocent. She lives for the moment, with no ulterior motive. She loses herself in the present and finds joy in simple pleasures. Her life is uncomplicated and devoid of distraction: she doesn't overthink things. The true athlete is a child, has a child's spirit, expresses a child's joy. She throws herself into the Game without care, without worry. She neither lusts for victory nor fears defeat. She plays the Game with all the ferocity, passion, and fire she can muster. And the chips fall where they may, not on her head, but at her agile and carefree feet.

# 69

# UNDERESTIMATION

Why shouldn't your opponent be just as talented as you? And just as motivated, just as persistent, just as resilient? Don't you realize that she's trying to accomplish the same goals, reach the same levels, experience the same joy? To underestimate what she's capable of is to undervalue the meaning of the competition itself, to undermine your own personal challenge. Give her the same credit you'd give yourself, expect of her the same courage and grit you expect from within you. After all, in that most famous of all athletic contests, remember what happened to the hare?

# 70

# INTUITION

What a miracle is the human brain! From its creases and crevices and ten billion neurons emerge the abilities to reason, ponder, opine, consider, examine, reflect, ratiocinate, contemplate, cogitate, meditate, ruminate, and deliberate. All at a moment's notice: but in a split second? *Useless!* You can't call on your intellect to react to the sudden bad hop and stab it in your webbing, to hit the half-volley topspin lob at the last possible second, to dart out into the passing lane—unannounced!—for the steal, to cut back against the grain on the spur of the moment, to perform the spontaneous deke or dink, to lunge instinctively for the impossible save. To perform these sporting flashes of genius, you rely on that certain something that comes deep from within. That ineffable, unnamable, unknowable, unthinking, and always dependable little voice that you follow obediently, that speaks to you in silent wisdom and shows you the light in the midst of the darkness. Neurons, shmeurons!

# 71

# PRESUMPTION

In the grand scheme of the Game, what can you presume to know or to understand? Who will win and who will lose? An enigma worthy of the Sphinx! How the ball will bounce? If you knew that, you could retire at eighteen and elect yourself into the Hall of Fame! How your opponent will perform under pressure? It's hard enough worrying about yourself! After years of playing, you'll no doubt improve, grow, and know yourself better. You'll also gain lots of experience and increase your enjoyment. But as far as understanding how it all works, the best time to gain any real insight is probably September 31.

# 72

# AWE

How awe-inspiring are the spectacular achievements of the human species! The great pyramids, Amiens Cathedral, the Sistine Ceiling, *King Lear*, Beethoven's Ninth! To say nothing of Wilt's 100, Joe's 56, Jack's 20, Mark's 7, Rod's 2! The common denominators between sports and art? Creativity and aspiration! Like the artist, the true athlete aspires, through hard work and persistence, to reach higher, push himself farther, and accomplish more every time he laces up the sneakers. Athletes of every age and size, look upon these feats in wonder!

# 73

# EASE

Athletic prowess that looks easy: the Grand Illusion of all time! Performing a feat with ease results not just from talent, but from perspiration and persistence. Like the magician who performs the seemingly effortless trick that follows thousands of hours of practice, the well-prepared athlete executes the ho-hum backward-layout-with-three-and-a-half-twists-in-the-pike-position or the pardon-me 650-pound-clean-and-jerk or the easy-does-it lunging-drop-volley-with-backspin only after endless hours of painfully tedious and repetitive drills. So don't believe the golfer who, when asked to comment on that nonchalant two-bounces-and-into-the-hole explosion shot from 60 yards against the wind from a bunker with a slightly-hooded sand wedge, replies, "Oh, it was nothing, really." It was *something!*

# 74

# CHANGE

What a kaleidoscope the Game is! Think of it: every day is a brand new day, with new challenges, new discoveries. Every shot is different, every pass, every pitch, every stroke, every jump, every stride! As conditions and opponents and sites change, you find new variations and ways to accommodate. Today's seven-iron is tomorrow's wedge. The power you used on cement needs to be transformed into touch on clay. There's rain in the forecast? Better change those cleats! The guy guarding you today is six inches taller than he was yesterday? Better adjust the arc in that jumper! And above all, never blink: you might miss something.

# 75

# AUTONOMY

How many crutches an athlete has at her disposal! She can be dependent on her coach, or her supporters or her teammates. She can find excuses in the condition of the field or of her own body. But when it's crunch time, who does she have but herself to look to? And what a blessing! After all, who's always there when she needs her? Who does she know any better? Who, more than herself, can she trust? Now if *you* had one person to count on, from the five billion or so available on the entire planet, who would it be?

# 76

# RESILIENCE

If you catch an egg properly *(pull hands back gently!)*, you'll begin to understand the importance of resilience. Sure, there's a time for power and hardness, but there's also a time for pliability and suppleness. The flip side of being strong is knowing how to yield. Do you know the most powerful tool you can use for draining a jumper or laying down a perfect bunt or hauling in a long bomb or executing an unreturnable drop shot? Why, it's the humble fingertip! You can't ski through a slalom pole or run through a baton pass. *Drive for show, putt for dough*. Follow the way of softness, and the egg will never crack.

# 77

## HUMILITY

No matter how outstanding you may fancy yourself to be, there's *always* someone better. No matter how satisfying your victory seems today, defeat is *always* hanging out, usually somewhere just around the corner. No matter how accomplished you may feel now, the Game will *always* put you in your proper place. And there are no exceptions. So if Ali *was* the greatest, why did he have to shout it to the world? If Namath *was* number one, why the need to flash the index finger? If Deion *was* a standout out on the ballroom floor, why the urge to do all that extra dancing? And if, after all those years, I finally *did* beat my father in our dollar Nassau, why did I feel compelled to nail the three bucks to the wall above my bed? Perhaps it's because we're all human. . . .

# 78

# FOCUS

The nice thing about being on the court or the course or the field is that . . . you're nowhere else! No bills to pay, no leaky faucet, just a service return. No dog to walk, no lawn to mow, just a six-foot putt. No meeting to prepare for, no commuting to work, just a grounder to gobble up. If you have nothing else to worry about, you can give all your attention to the moment. If you can block out before and after, you can concentrate on *now*. Which, after all, is fitting: it's where all the action is!

# 79

# FAILURE

Would you rather win and stay the same than lose and grow? Would you rather crush a weak opponent than learn from losing to a strong one? In every contest, at any given moment, mistakes are made, opportunities missed: the nature of performance under pressure. You fail, you lose, you come up short constantly, even in victory. How to correct errors, how to learn from defeat, how to know weaknesses for the next time—*that* is the great challenge. The joy that comes from winning will pass; the joy that comes from insight will endure. And the only person truly aware of this is the one looking right back at you when you look straight at him. You know, the guy in the mirror.

# 80

# CONTENTMENT

Are you happy with who you are? Do you look outside for approval? Are your wishes to excel, to grow, and to improve stronger than your thoughts of victory, superiority, and control? The athlete who's happy with herself can be content with whatever the Game has to offer: adversity, rewards, surprise, even winning and losing. She can accept results not with disappointment and ecstasy, but with calm and gratitude. She can view the efforts of her opponent not with scorn, but with compassion. If she's happy with herself, she'll be content with outside events, however glorious or dismal they may appear: she has found the center. She can stand back and look at the bouncing ball with equanimity, even amusement: she's at home with the Game. Emerson was in agreement: *Nothing can bring you peace but yourself.*

# 81

# SACRIFICE

In sports, as in life, it's better to give than to receive. Why? Because there's always something more important than the Self. For the individual player, there's the competition: he's not giving just to himself but to his opponent as well, raising the level of the contest, increasing the joy of the battle. For the team player, there's the team: giving up selfish individual goals in order to contribute to shared collective ones is the true way to self-satisfaction. And for all players, there's the Game: giving oneself up to the Game is the highest ideal to which an athlete can commit himself. Learn this, and the Game will give everything back to you. And much more.

# ACKNOWLEDGMENTS

I'd like to express my gratitude to a number of people who contributed to this book, knowingly or unknowingly. To Mike Appelbaum and John Hubner, for their kind words of support and encouragement. To Richard Grossinger, for believing in the concept and for sensing that the acorn proposal I submitted to him might become an oak someday. To Lindy Hough for her sensitive shepherding, to Paula Morrison for her tasteful design, and to Kathy Glass for her acute and sensible editing. To Stephen Mitchell, who read the unfinished manuscript using a comb with excruciatingly fine teeth (and of course for his fraternal affection). To my children, Noah, Jennifer, and Sarah, for their love. And to my best friend, Diane, for hers.

## ABOUT THE AUTHOR

Bob Mitchell was born in Brooklyn in 1944 and studied at Williams, Columbia, and Harvard, where he received a Ph.D. in French and Comparative Literature. He was a French professor for eleven years at Harvard, Purdue, and Ohio State, during which time he published four books on nineteenth- and twentieth-century French poetry. He entered advertising in 1981 as a copywriter, became a Creative Director at a number of New York agencies, and spent 1994 in Tel Aviv as a special consultant on commercial film writing and production. Since then, he has been spending his time writing books about his first love—sports.

Passionate about sports, as both spectator and participant, he has followed all major and minor sports since 1951, lettered in three sports at Williams College (soccer, squash, tennis), and has taught tennis professionally.

Mitchell is the author of a book of poems entitled *The Heart Has Its Reasons: Reflections on Sports and Life.* He lives in Sonoma, California, with his best friend, Diane, and his dog, Maglie.